12 Steps to
Deep Inner Healing

Expand Your Spirituality

These teachings are designed to trigger your ability to open your mind and spirit to reveal a clearer perception of yourself, and open you for healing and improved connection to spirit. Just 20 minutes a day for two weeks will begin a journey that can and will transform your life.

David Nelmes

http://www.DeepHealingLight.com

http://www.HealingTouchShoppe.com

12 Steps to Deep Inner Healing
Expand Your Spirituality

Contents

Preface

I spent a large portion of my life believing that somehow my issues were dramatically associated with just myself, since who else could possibly have the complexities in their mind like I did. Over time, though, I realized that many, if not most people, had similar thoughts about how their issues or problems seemed uniquely associated with themselves.

Once it became clearer that I was not an enigma and somehow could relate on a deeper level with those around me, my natural reaction was to find ways to be helpful to them, because knowing how screwed up my mind was, I could only want to extend help to those around me, and hopefully within the process, learn more about myself.

Because of this desire to be truly helpful for the past 20 years, I feel I have grown spiritually to a place I had not imagined possible in the past. With all the issues presenting themselves, time and time again, I kept working on being open and kept truly desiring that I would allow that which was best, and that heartfelt desire has brought me to this place today, with you.

Being a man that likes rhythm or structure, I often find myself ironing out methods or thought systems that are helpful to me in my journey back to source. I'll write down a page or two of things I might like to remember to include during a meditation or what I would like to introduce in my next reiki session. This pattern of creating pathways or systems is what has led me to create this book about Inner Healing.

Knowing that many of the things that I have faced, others may be facing as well, I took the best aspects of what I learned and have performed myself, and created a easy to understand and follow set of daily sessions that almost anyone could understand and choose to follow.

I have extended a sincere intention that everyone who follows the steps provided in this book will be helped by spirit, every moment and every step of the way. Not only will you not be alone, but you will be supported, guided and lead as you work through this healing process of your inner spirit and mind.

But knowing also that you are a unique being, and that maybe not everything I am teaching will resonate with you, I extend a sincere intention that regardless of what I am teaching here, that you will experience a healing that which is best for you, and have the epiphanies and awakenings that are perfect, and waiting for you.

Namaste

Introduction

Healing is the result of allowing errors to be undone. Since we are all perfect creations in our true form, our perception of our existence here is simply an error in how we have accepted ourselves. So, if we were to open our mind and spirit to see ourselves for who we really are, healing would take place.

These 12 Steps to Deep Inner Healing are designed to trigger your ability to open your mind and spirit to reveal a clearer perception of yourself and open you for inner healing and improved connection to spirit.

Just 20 minutes a day for two weeks will begin a journey that can and will transform your life. You will eventually do this someday. **Why not now?**

This book is broken into 12 daily sessions. It is suggested you do no more than one session per day, since this both encourages and allows you to absorb the teachings while having opportunity to practice them or set things in place.

Each session includes deeper information on methods and ideas that will help you gain a greater capacity to free yourself of many of your current limitations of mind and will lead you on a path to daily healing. Each session also includes a task for the day to place the new ideas into action, a helpful quote for gaining further insight and a list of suggested accessories that might help in completing that step more easily.

Once complete, you can use these sessions in whole or in part as a template for how you interact with spirit for the rest of your life, or until a clearer direction or perception presents itself. Nothing is changeless, so even what I teach here is simply what I believe is currently best, so this is a wonderful place for you to start and evolve into what works best for you.

Although you can work your way through the book in just under two weeks, to obtain the highest possible results, it would be best to perform the steps a second time and to find ways to permanently include certain aspects of these teachings into your daily thoughts and meditations.

Step #1 - Creating a Quiet Time and Space

There is never a reason to think something must be done a certain way or at a certain time. This would promote anxiety or fear of missing something, so whenever an idea is presented here, especially when having to do with time, see it as a helpful suggestion, and not as a rule or law.

Overall, when looking to enter a prayer or meditative state, it is much better to ensure you will have a quiet and undisturbed period of time set aside. Again, not pivotal, but very helpful.

Quiet could be absolute silence, or if you are like me, I get easily distracted by neighborhood sounds, so I like to play Reiki or meditative music in the background to mask out any outward noises. Jonathan Goldman is one of my favorite artists. A link to suggested music is provided later in this chapter.

To be truly undisturbed, it is best to find a place behind a closed door if possible, so that you genuinely feel you can just be yourself and relax. To give you a nice idea of this setting, I have included an image of my meditation room. I also use this room to provide Reiki sessions and perform my distance healings from here. The bottom line is that I created a space where I feel comfortable, welcome and free to be myself. To ensure your mind could fully relax, it is also helpful to either remove or shut off any mobile phone, so that the possibility of disturbance doesn't even exist.

I recommend that you remain seated, so that you would not easily fall to sleep, but this doesn't mean to not be comfortable. I have found that using a nice cushioned chair works best for me. It provides the comfort and support I need to feel comfortable, plus it aids me in sitting more upright which can aid in the energy flow through your being. Sitting upright also provides the opportunity to keep your feet rested on the floor, helping with grounding and releasing old or used energy. Regardless, there is no magic wand associated with how you sit or choose to lay dawn. The only important thing is that you enter a relaxed place where you will remain conscious.

Today's Task:

If you don't already have a comfortable and quiet place to meditate, set up a place now. If you like background music, load the music on your computer, MP3 or Bluetooth player and have everything ready so there is no last-minute rushing around later. You want to experience peace, so being better prepared reduces chaos and promotes peace.

I provide multiple references to products I have already purchased for myself and have found to be reliable and helpful in setting up my meditation space. Although not necessary, they can be helpful in creating an atmosphere that helps you relax and acquire a greater capacity to focus.

Today's quote from ACIM:

"Each day should be devoted to miracles. The purpose of time is to enable man to learn to use it constructively. Time is thus a teaching device and a means to an end." – ACIM T-1.I.15:1-3

Recommended Accessories and Services:

A Course in Miracles - Original Edition

Note: *A Course in Miracles is somewhat of a base upon how I see things. If you haven't read it, I highly recommend you do. I prefer the original version.*

The great classic work, A Course in Miracles, is devoted to teachings about who we are, our relationships to God and with each other, and the mental nature of our bodies and the world.

There are three constituent parts to the Course: The Text, a Workbook for Students, and the Manual for Teachers. The Text lays out the theoretical foundation for the metaphysical system of the Course. The Workbook contains a series of 365 Lessons to be practiced daily for the purpose of retraining the mind and healing our perception.

Himalayan Pink Salt Lamp Basket

I always keep a salt lamp on in the background. In addition to the pleasing aesthetics it adds to a room, it helps to purify and ionize the air. I also like that it acts as a night-light or a nice background light for meditation or reiki sessions.

Portable Bluetooth Stereo Speaker

I set up one of these in my meditation / reiki room. Although it's Bluetooth, I also liked that it had a USB port for a flash drive, so I copied my favorite meditation and reiki session albums onto a flash drive and this has been playing in the background 24/7 at low volume for almost a year now .

I thought it would be helpful, or even important that the room I chose to perform my meditations and Reiki sessions would be immersed in a constant frequency of healing and loving sound, and I will admit that the room has a different feel than the other rooms in my home. When you enter, it is immediately serene.

Jonathan Goldman: Frequencies – Sounds of Healing

Jonathan Goldman is my direct fallback for what I listen to during meditation and Reiki sessions. He is a world-renowned authority in the field of sound healing who presents lectures, workshops and intensive training sessions around the world.

This album, Frequencies: Sounds of Healing, is a collection of excerpts from award-winning and best-selling Spirit Music recordings. Each is a positive tool for transformation. Includes ancient and culturally diverse sacred sounds, cutting-edge psycho-acoustic frequencies, solo/group toning & chanting, musical textures, and dolphin songs to provide listeners with a wide variety of aural tools for healing and transformation.

Nag Champa Incense

Of all the incense brands out there, I feel that the Nag Champa brand is of higher quality than many others, plus I like the style of their variety, having selections such as 'Reiki', 'Spiritual Healing', 'Chakra', 'Namaste', 'Positive Vibes', and so many more.

Each stick last around 45 minutes and not only takes care of the room it is in but works its way through the entire home as well.

If you do not already have the accessories listed, you can get more information about them on our website at:

http://www.deephealinglight.com/healing-services/courses/12-step-deep-healing-accessories.php

Notes

_____

_____

_____

_____

_____

_____

_____

_____

_____

_____

_____

_____

_____

_____

Step #2 - Settling Thoughts and Relaxing

We often don't realize how active our brains are until we try to stop the whirring of activity in our heads. It is necessary for you to create a new focus that helps eliminate all the other noise.

So, what do you focus on? It helps to choose a word or an image that you make a central point in your mind. It could be a bright white light, the word "*Peace*", or whatever comes to mind that helps you relax and feel good.

Even the most well-intentioned person can find their mind wandering after just seconds of having chosen to focus on quiet. Eventually you will become better at not losing focus, but for now, the most important thing is to choose to be vigilant in regaining focus more quickly.

Our minds wander. It's what they do, but we are not helpless in this. We can choose to be focused. The best way to go about this is to not consciously fight the thoughts coming in. Let them come in but be aware of them. See them almost from an outside point of view.

Your mind has so many things that it is always trying to do, so when you choose to quiet your mind, it initially sees it as an opportunity to get things done that it couldn't do when you were being busy, so let it. When you first close your eyes to begin a meditation or prayer session, let the thoughts flow through. Let them finish, but don't add to them. Don't initiate plans or new thoughts, just let the ones that are already there finish up.

Your initial challenge is to not get easily distracted by something you did forget about earlier that now pops into your head, or issues and concerns of the day that have not been resolved. Just let the thoughts slide past. You are not ignoring them, you are just saying, "*Thank-you, we'll take care of that later*".

During this time, you also want to start relaxing your body. This will work to help clear your thoughts as well since your relaxed body will send different signal to your brain, triggering different thoughts. A less stressful body sends less stressful thoughts.

You don't realize how tense your body is until you create a focus to relax it. Sit back for a moment and pay momentary attention to your facial muscles and choose to relax them. Do this same thing for your neck and shoulders, and then your upper body and then the legs and feet. It's amazing how much tension we have become accustomed to.

As much as this may be necessary to perform activities throughout your day, it's not helpful during meditation, so you want to let the tension go.

Today's Task:

Go to your quiet space, close your eyes, relax your body muscles one area at a time, starting from the head, working down, and select your focus image and/or word. Keep this word or image in your mind and gradually let your other thoughts pass by ... *"I'll get you later"*. Just be quiet and appreciate now. No pressure, no demands, just now.

Today's Quote from ACIM:

"Prayer is the medium of miracles. Prayer is the natural communication of the created with the Creator. Through prayer love is received, and through miracles love is expressed." – ACIM T-1.I.11

Recommended Accessories

There are many authors on Amazon who have written short e-books and paperback books that might provide you with more in-depth procedures about how to quiet your mind. If you perform today's task several times and still can't quiet your mind, we have provided additional options at: http://www.deephealinglight.com/healing-services/courses/12-step-deep-healing-accessories.php

Notes

_____

_____

_____

_____

_____

_____

_____

_____

_____

_____

_____

_____

_____

_____

Step #3 - Clearing Your Energy and Chakras

For your meditation or prayers to have their greatest effectiveness, it can be very helpful to clear hindering or unhelpful energy from your being, as well as reestablishing the energy flow through your chakras and setting them in balance at the same time.

The first step is to release unhelpful energy. This is energy that has been depleted, or unhelpful energy absorbed from activities and other people. This energy, as we hold onto it, makes it more and more difficult for us to accomplish things in our lives. It literally clogs up our capacity to perform, mentally, physically and spiritually.

The next step is to then restore your chakras and realign your energy flow throughout your being.

You have seven chakras

1. – Root - red, located at the base of the spine

2. – Sacral - orange, located below the naval

3. – Solar Plexus - yellow, located on your abdomen or naval

29

4. – Heart - green, located on the middle of your chest

5. – **Throat** - blue, located on your neck and throat

6. – **Third Eye** - indigo, located just above your eyebrows, between your eyes

7. – Crown - violet, located just above your head

Energy flows into them from the top, #7, all the way through to the bottom #1. Re-establishing this energy flow has more benefits than I am going to explain here, but let's just say the benefits are physical, emotional, spiritual, and metaphysical.

Today's Task:

To clear your energy, envision an anchor that goes deep into the Earth, with a line coming up right below you. Plant your feet flat on the ground if possible and envision that you are standing on this grounding mat that has connected yourself to this spiritual grounding system.

What you want to do next is to loosen your grip on your being by relaxing every muscle you can feel, then starting from your head and working down to your feet, you want to release and return this energy to the earth.

Be thankful for how the energy served you, and now it's time to let it go. It just takes a few seconds to just let it go, return to Mother Earth and be recycled for another use, another way, another day.

Next, you work on clearing your chakras. Start with #7 and work your way down to #1. For each chakra, imagine a vibrant white light illuminating above you. Physically breathe in through your nose while also visualizing that white light being absorbed into your body from above. Breathe in the air while also breathing in the light.

Hold your breath for just a second and as you exhale through your nose or mouth, exhale energy through that chakra as well, clearing, cleansing and restoring balance to that chakra. Do this at least three times for each chakra.

When you are finished, take a moment and allow the energy to flow in from above and flow out of every part of you... through your fingers, toes, elbows, feet, hands or wherever you can take a moment to imagine ... and let yourself feel it happening, revitalizing you and preparing you to better handle your day.

If you find that any specific chakra is difficult to clear or you simply prefer to work with crystals and aromas to help with clearing the chakras, a Chakra Healing Kit (https://www.healingtouchshoppe.com/collections/chakra-healing-kits/) has been developed that will provide you with the tools and helpful affirmations to help you truly dig into and heal that chakra. Learn more about Deep Healing Light's Chakra Healing Kits at (https://www.healingtouchshoppe.com/collections/chakra-healing-kits/)

Today's Quote from ACIM:

"Miracles reawaken the awareness that the spirit, not the body, is the altar of truth. This is the recognition that leads to the healing power of the miracle." – ACIM T-1.I.20

Recommended Accessories:

16 x 20 Chakra Chart Poster - Chakra Girl

I couldn't image my meditation room without having Chakra Girl on the wall. This is a visually pleasing poster, plus it provides affirmations specific for each Chakra, so during meditating or Reiki, when you notice an issue pertaining to any chakra, simply look to Chakra Girl and read that affirmation several times, letting it sink in.

Benjia Magnetic Poster Hanger

I found it's the best way to hang the Chakra Girl poster on the wall. It consists of several wooden strips that have magnets on them, so it grabs the poster and provides weight to keep it straight.

LandKissing® Grounding Mats Kit

I like that this kit came with two mats. I placed one on the floor in front of my meditation room chair and placed the other at the foot of the Reiki bed. Now, while meditating or providing a Reiki session, grounding is simply built into the process.

If you do not already have the accessories listed, you can get more information about them on our website at:
http://www.deephealinglight.com/healing-services/courses/12-step-deep-healing-accessories.php

Notes

Step #4 - Connecting with Guides, Ascended Masters and Angels

There is never and has never been a split second of time where you were alone or abandoned or forgotten. Although we have all felt like

that at some point, it still doesn't make it true. You are surrounded by guides, angels, masters, family, friends, and other beings beyond count. They exist in a different plane and therefore, are not readily accessible to see or hear, but this doesn't really matter, because they are still there.

You may have asked: *Why does it matter to connect? What difference would it make? Is it possible to actually connect?*

There is no single answer to any of these questions other than to say we are not separate from anyone or anything, and this includes the spirit(s) that surrounds us. We are all here to help each other. There is nothing owed. There is nobody or no thing that is obligated to be helpful, since being helpful is a natural state of being. You don't have to ask for help, you simply have to allow it. So that is what you will learn to do, to allow help, intervention and communication from your guides and any being of light that would be helpful interacting with you.

Don't misunderstand this process as being similar to allowing in lower level spirits into your being. The reality is that just because a being is no longer physical, doesn't mean they have ascended and have the pursuit of truth, peace, love and light at the center of their being. Many spirits are at lower levels. They are not necessarily harmful or malicious, but their perspectives and guidance could be tainted with wounded motivations because they still are not whole yet themselves.

Keep that in mind whenever anyone says they have a message from spirit. You cannot be hurt by listening but take what you hear and ask if it comes from a place of love or fear; a place of peace or anger; a place of patience or urgency. Higher, ascended or lighter spirits extend only love, peace and patience, so if you hear anything different, just let it go and know that it may not be a valid message to follow or react to.

When you connect to spirit, your focus will be to connect to spirits of light, ascended masters, angels of light, your own higher self and assigned guides. You will specifically ask for those spirits and guides and none other can gain access without your consent, so there is nothing to fear or be concerned about.

Aids you can use to better connect to spirit includes the use of oracle or tarot cards, and the use of pendulums. A link to a few select items that I believe can be helpful is provided later in this chapter.

Today's Task:

For the most part, all you have to do is to welcome and allow spirits of light to interact with you. You can say to yourself, *"I'd like to welcome my (higher self, or guides, or angels of light, or ascended masters, etc.) to speak to me, and help me with the decisions I make or am trying to make. I allow you to be a part of my life, and truly do welcome you and extend my gratitude that you are there for me, and that I am truly never alone."* ... or something along that line. Repeat it a few times and work on truly being open for it.

After making this offer, allow yourself to be still and clear your mind as much as possible, entering just the edge of your sleep or dream state and see if you can stay there, and just listen for what they have to say. You might hear words, you might see images, or you might feel an emotion. Allow yourself to be patient. Maybe nothing will happen at all, but if you experience that while being patient, you will simply try again later. Your patience will provide you with the capacity to continue to practice until it feels normal to simply connect with spirit.

Today's quote from ACIM:

"Miracles as such do not matter. The only thing that matters is their Source, which is far beyond human evaluation." – ACIM T-1.I.2

Recommended Accessories and Services:

Daily Guidance from Your Angels Oracle Cards

This 44-card deck offers comforting and uplifting messages, to set a positive and healing tone for the day. It also functions as a divination tool, as you can ask a question and find the message that gives you guidance and answers. This work is designed to help you stay centered in peacefulness throughout the day, and to remember that your angels are always beside you, ready to help you with every area of your life.

Energy Oracle Cards

The Energy Oracle Cards are designed to reveal both the present energy you project and the results you are likely to attract.

These easy-to-use cards will help you understand what your consciousness is creating, as well as reveal any hidden blocks that may be delaying your progress. The information they bring will empower and inspire you, for it comes from heavenly messengers, friends from the spirit realm and your own higher self.

Natural Lapis Gemstone Hexagonal Reiki Chakra Pendulum

I would recommend that whether you actively make use of a pendulum or not, that you still get one so that it is there for when the time is right to begin using it.

These can be highly helpful with getting information from spirit or for helping to determine the condition of chakras during a Reiki session.

How to Use a Pendulum: 9 Secrets for Accurate Answers

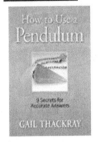

This is a comprehensive book written on the subject of pendulums. Great in-depth instructions on how to use a pendulum to read people, divine the future, discover health issues and much more. This is great for total beginner as well as professional readers.

Provides many tips and unique methods you won't learn anywhere else. Includes a chart to use to determine past lives and divine questions. Also includes tips to discover which pendulums work best for you and how to clear your pendulum and reset it when you get unclear answers.

If you do not already have the accessories listed, you can get more information about them on our website at: http://www.deephealinglight.com/healing-services/courses/12-step-deep-healing-accessories.php

Notes

_____

_____

_____

_____

_____

_____

_____

_____

_____

_____

_____

_____

_____

_____

_____

_____

Step #5 - Accepting Yourself as Being Worthy

We are not alone in what we perceive or believe to be true. What this means is that what we believe is true or inevitable for others, will also be true or inevitable for yourself. This means that as long as you see others as less than the true gifts they are; you will never experience the true gift that you are as well. What you believe about others, you believe for yourself and what you believe about yourself, you also believe for others.

In some ways, your greatest gift is the person next to you, or anyone you think of at this moment, whether near or far. Can you see them for the child of God they are? Can you see they are totally worthy of anything and everything our Creator would provide? What you allow yourself to see in them, you can also be open to see in yourself.

Our history is full of instances where people have brought harm to others because they were different, whether it is the color of their skin, their language, their beliefs or their political preferences. This circumstance would never exist if we saw others as they truly were in the eyes of our Creator. If you cannot or are unwilling to see them as being totally worthy, you will not be able to see yourself as being worthy either, regardless of how you might think otherwise.

Feeling superior is not the same as being worthy. Feeling above somebody is not the same as being worthy. Feeling better than somebody is not the same as being worthy. Being worthy is about embracing the concept that worthiness is unilateral, across the board and applies to everyone, including you.

When any part of us feels unworthy, no matter the reason, it increases the density between us and any being who is there to aid us in our journey. That angel, master, guide, etc., never chooses to not be helpful, but they are limited in how they can help because they honor the walls we build around ourselves. We created them, not anyone else, so only we can allow them to be penetrated or undone.

For anyone looking to walk more deeply with spirit and have real results with respect to resolving life's problems, you must see yourself as being worthy, and you are. We all are. When you see yourself as being worthy, you make it so much easier for energy to flow between you and any being choosing to help you. This is a very helpful concept to grab onto and work on until it feels true.

Today's Task:

Say to yourself, phrases similar to what follows:

- *"I am as loved by God as anyone or anything."*

- "*I am worthy of all the abundance, health and blessings the universe has to offer.*"

- "*I am pure and totally worthy to stand before God and not be ashamed or feel uninvited. God created me and has never stopped loving me and honoring me.*"

- "*My brother or sister, or annoying neighbor are all equally worthy.*"

- "*Everyone I ever heard of, know now, will ever meet or hear of, are totally worthy beings of our Source Creator.*"

- "*My worthiness is not based upon anything I did or will do because it's not possible to establish my worthiness on my own. God established it once and forever, the moment I was created.*"

See yourself standing before God, set aside any thought of anything you believe might diminish your image of yourself, and just know that God's only thought at that moment is: "*Behold, my child, in whom I am well pleased.*"

Today's quote from ACIM:

"*The miracle dissolves error because the Spiritual eye identifies error as false or unreal. This is the same as saying that by perceiving light, darkness automatically disappears.*" – ACIM T-1.I.40

Recommended Accessories:

101 "*I AM*" Power Affirmations

Affirmations are an incredibly powerful tool, and when used correctly, they will change your life. What is unique about this book is all 101 Affirmations are original and start with "*I AM*" and the reason for this i because "*I Am*" are the two most powerful words known to man because whatever you say after them will determine how you think an feel about yourself. It influences your ability to function in the world and the quality of the future that you create for yourself because your words create your reality.

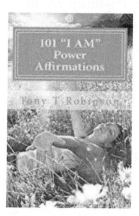

"*I AM*" is the essence of who you are! Whatever you say after that will either greatly improve the quality of your life or quickly diminish it. By starting your sentence with "*I AM*" you are in effect supercharging your affirmation with additional power because when you say those tw words you are speaking directly to the core of wh you are and if you want to change or improve an area of your life these affirmations in this format will help to facilitate that change.

If you do not already have the accessory listed, you can get more information about it on our website at:
http://www.deephealinglight.com/healing-services/courses/12-step-deep-healing-accessories.php

Notes

_____

_____

_____

_____

_____

_____

_____

_____

_____

_____

_____

_____

_____

_____

Step #6 - Releasing Bindings, Bonds, Agreements, and Contracts

It is very likely you can recall moments where you reacted a certain way to something, but you really don't know why you reacted the way you did. It's very possible the seeds for those decisions come from programming you created or simply accepted at some point in your existence.

During your current life and during other past lives and existences, you often came to conclusions that some things are to be a certain way. You made these agreements with yourself, both consciously and unconsciously, and many of these agreements, contracts, bindings or bonds are still a part of you, and may be affecting you in unhelpful ways.

For example, an unconscious agreement could be one where you had an experience where you fell off a high place and either got hurt badly or even died. If, when that happened, you concluded that high places are dangerous, that thought could stay with you forever, lifetime after lifetime, until you undo it. Meanwhile, you may feel uncomfortable or even terrified of high places, without having any idea why. You just are.

Similarly, a drowning experience could have left you with a fear of water; a brutal relationship could leave you with feelings of low self-esteem; an untimely death of any kind could instill a fear associated with the manner in which that happened ... and the list goes on and on. All these previous experiences could leave breadcrumbs that affect decisions we make about anything, at any point in any day, and we would not normally see where that motivation comes from.

In the same frame of thinking, a conscience agreement would be similar, with the exception that you made the choice deliberately. This could be as simple as having said that you get sick every winter, or that people are out to get you. These things can stay with you until you undo them and let them go.

As with unconscious agreements, conscious agreements could also be from past lives where you concluded that something was a certain way because you were weak or stupid or any unhelpful thought along that line, and you could just as easily carry this thinking into lives that follow.

You don't have to know what these conscious agreements or contracts are to undo them, but it does help to be somewhat aware that there is a potential issue in the first place so that you choose to take the time to release them.

Today's Task:

For generic agreements of which you are not aware, simply say something along the line:

"Any unhelpful agreements, contracts or bindings that I made in either this existence or another, I release them and hand them over to spirit. I created them, so I cherished them and held onto them, but I choose to now release them. "

Similarly, for a specific item you are aware you are having an issue with, say something like this:

"The agreement I made about _____, I release it and hand it over to spirit. I created it, so I cherished it and held onto it, but I choose to now release it. "

or

"Any agreement I made that affects why I am having trouble with _____, I release it and hand it over to spirit. I created it, so I cherished it and held onto it, but I choose to now release it. "

As you make those statements, allow yourself to feel the energy shift when you do this. Pull in energy from above, and let it wash through you and release this back to the universe through the air in your breathe as you speak these commands.

Repeat this process several times overall, and for every specific thing you can think of. Take your time, relax, close your eyes and allow yourself to become aware of where you are tripping over something in your life that you can apply to this exercise.

Today's quote from ACIM:

"Miracles are natural expressions of total forgiveness. Through miracles, man accepts God's forgiveness by extending it to others." – ACIM T-1.I.21

Notes

_____

_____

_____

_____

_____

_____

_____

_____

_____

_____

_____

_____

_____

_____

Step #7 - Releasing Your Base Guilt and Fear

You are guilty of nothing, and therefore, have nothing to fear.

One of my favorite self-quotes is:

"God is a God of unconditional Love and He does not teach through fear or use fear in any way."

This is the basis for re-identifying our true place before our creator. The root of any fear is based upon our concept of retribution in some form, and the base for this concept is in our base idea of who or what God is and what we believe he wants to do to us. To release our guilt and fears, we must first release our image of a fearful God.

Our perception of God as being something to fear is

often based upon what the Bible and many ancient texts taught us. The only reason things appear that way is because our fear convinced us to choose to use these references in a way that created bondage and stunted our spiritual growth, instead of using them as steppingstones. There are truths in the Bible and other ancient texts, but they were never meant to be taken word for word...for thousands of years.

Imagine if you were still reading the book about 'Spot'. Your vocabulary and writing skills would be limited to things such as "*See Spot run*". All that you knew and were capable of understanding would be limited to that one book. If you believed that was the only book to reference and only the words in that book mattered, you would have grown to a certain level and just stopped...not growing for ages...so determined that only that book was the book to follow. To defend your book, you would have to denounce all other books that were different than yours. Things that did not make sense in your book would be rationalized over and over again as the ages went by...in attempts to preserve what you believe is the only source of truth. You would have to purposely not allow any other truth into your life because it was not allowed to show anything different than your book.

Now, take a look at the Bible or any other ancient text. These books were vital and necessary to bring order and a sense of God to a world that had multiple gods. The information in these books was perfect for the people of its time, but this information was never supposed to be set aside as the "*end all be all*" words of God. God never stopped communicating and God never just communicated through a single book or two. What you are reading now are words from God...no more or less valuable than any words in the Bible or any other text inspired by God.

God is on your side...no matter what your race...no matter what your religion...no matter who you are...no matter what you have done...no matter where you live...no matter what you eat...no matter what physical laws you have broken...no matter what you think of God...no matter whether you are seeking him or not...no matter whether you believe in him or not...no matter what. There is no condition God has set to love you. You can't earn it or lose it....it's just there.

Now, if you can imagine that this is true, then you have no reason to fear God for any reason, and without fear, guilt cannot exist. Fear is a choice. Guilt is a choice. You can make a different choice.

Today's Task:

Close your eyes and see yourself standing before your Source, creator, God or however you wish to identify your creator being. Accept and know that you are loved beyond description. Accept and know that you are always held and cared for. Allow the light and love of your creator to fill your being and visualize all your fear and guilt as a dark little ball within yourself and let it rise up out of you, into his light, and see that dark ball simply vanish as its darkness ceases to exist in the light.

In whatever form seems comfortable, or comes to mind, say this, or something like this:

"God's love for me is without conditions. He does not judge me in any way. He is not holding me accountable for anything. His eternal patience assures me that I have all the time necessary to return to him some day, so there is nothing to fear, and likewise, nothing to feel guilty about."

Today's quote from ACIM:

"Miracles are both beginnings and endings. They thus alter the temporal order. They are always affirmations of rebirth which seem to go back but really go forward. They undo the past in the present and thus release the future." – ACIM T-1.I.13

Recommended Accessories and Services:

Seeing God: Perhaps for The First Time

Is God a God of love or a God of fear? I believe God is a God of unconditional love, so this book was written to clearly show that God is a God of love and that He does not teach through fear or use fear in any way.

The pursuit of truth never ends, and what appears to be a vital truth today, may just be a breadcrumb to an even clearer perceived truth. With this in mind, I am saying that you should never set anything so solidly as being true because when you do this, you may purposely oppose or run from other breadcrumbs that can be very helpful, simply because they do not appear to line up with your current concept of truth.

Over the 10 years where I wrote these articles, many of my perceptions and motivations have cleared or improved, reversing or scaling back the importance of some aspects of the articles as compared to when I originally wrote them. This is wonderful since this clearly illustrates growth towards openness rather than steadfast retaining of assumed truths. In my commentaries, where this shift has occurred, I help explain the shift and provide insight to see what brought upon the change.

If you do not already have the accessory listed, you can get more information about it on our website at: http://www.deephealinglight.com/healing-services/courses/12-step-deep-healing-accessories.php

---

After purchasing the above title, please do consider providing an honest review on Amazon about how it did or did not help you, or any thoughts about the book you would like to share.

Namaste

Notes

Step #8 - Handing Over Thoughts to (Holy) Spirit for Correction

Throughout our day, our life, or lives, we often think poorly of ourselves and others. These thoughts hinder us, and they can make it

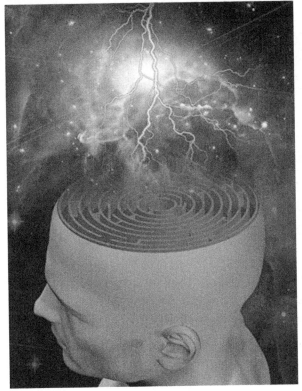

more difficult for others as well. True thought that stems from unconditional love, spawns' creation. Our thoughts that stem from a fear-based existence, spawns' errors in perception and builds walls to our capacity to see things or understand things as they really are.

We are not alone in our thinking. What we believe or think about yourself will also apply to all those around you, and what you think about all those around you will apply to you. It is totally true that the only real way to help yourself is to help another, because it will always return to help you because you will experience what you share.

Thoughts either support or hinder yourself and others. For example, a thought that you are unpleasant or even unlovable, can result in sadness, or secluding oneself. While a thought that you are very capable, can result in a great feeling throughout your day.

The thing about thoughts is that they create our overall experience. If you limit the worthiness of a brother, you then believe unworthiness is real, and this thought will then also apply to you. If you bless your brothers, you will believe blessings are real, and you will be open to receive them as well.

A Course in Miracles states:

"I am responsible for what I see. I choose the feelings I experience, and I decide upon the goal I would achieve. And everything that seems to happen to me, I ask for, and receive as I have asked."

Our thoughts are more powerful than what we can image. Our experience here is created by them, so by learning to become more aware of your thoughts, you can change your experience for the best.

Thoughts are helpful or unhelpful, but never good nor bad as we have been taught. I believe it is best to be helpful whenever possible, so the less unhelpful thoughts that exist, it helps us all. To release your thoughts that are unhelpful, you simply hand them over to spirit to correct. What this means is that spirit will take that thought and either totally release it back to source or refashion it and return it to you in a helpful way.

Once you release an unhelpful thought, you want to set something in its place or the original frame of thinking can more easily return, so after having released a thought, it can be very helpful to set a helpful opposite thought or positive affirmation in its place.

For example:

- if you were to hand over hate, your affirmation would be to embrace love instead

- if you were to hand over being cruel, your affirmation would be to be kind instead

- if you were to hand over stealing, your affirmation would be to embrace honesty instead

Release the unhelpful and embrace a higher choice.

By filling this void of what you handed over, not only have you released something that isn't helpful, but you have chosen to embrace something that is. That choice is a powerful one, and it brings great healing to the core of your being.

Today's Task:

Spend a few moments and think about where you are making judgements about yourself or others that do not seem to be helpful thoughts and hand them over to spirit to correct, and then follow up with a helpful affirmation.

You could say:

"This thought I had about _____,

I hand over to spirit to correct.

I would rather I embraced _____ instead".

Apply this to any thought that appears questionable with respect to it having been a loving thought or not. If the thoughts were not loving, hand them over.

Repeat this process several times until you can't find anything to hand over, then, remember this process and use it every day or every week, forever, to keep unhelpful thoughts from growing within.

Today's quote from ACIM:

"A miracle is a correction factor introduced into false thinking by me. It acts as a catalyst, shaking up erroneous perception and reorganizing it properly. This places man under the Atonement principle, where his perception is healed." – ACIM T-1.I.38:1-3

Recommended Products and Services:

Breaking Through When Feeling Stuck: And Not Getting Stuck Again

When you find yourself stuck in a situation where you feel as though the same unhelpful cycles repeat over and over again; and you can't seem to put your finger on what is wrong or how to even start to get unstuck... you need a real solution to break through and help prevent it from happening again. You need a real solution from somebody who went through the same thing and truly did find a way to break through. That's why I wrote this book.

Who will be helped the most by this book? If you have been feeling stuck in any aspect of your life, like with your job, finances, weight, stress, troubled relationships or your spirituality overall, you can transform your life by following the '**Breaking Through**' process that teaches you how to peel back, expose and resolve your issues once and for all.

Even if you are not feeling stuck but just have a few spiritual blocks you would like to clear away, the '**Breaking Through**' process will help you take care of them as well.

Overall, if you ever find you are asking yourself, "***Why am I stuck? How do I get unstuck? What do I have to do to stop feeling stuck?***", this book helps you find your answers by teaching you how to get to the root of your problems so that you can truly fix them and prevent them from coming back again.

If you do not already have the accessory listed, you can get more information about it on our website at:
http://www.deephealinglight.com/healing-services/courses/12-step-deep-healing-accessories.php

---

After purchasing the above title, please do consider providing an honest review on Amazon about how it did or did not help you, or any thoughts about the book you would like to share.

Namaste

67

Notes

Step #9 - Following Threads

A Course in Miracles states that, *"We are never upset for the reason we think"*. This means there is always something behind our thoughts and actions that are driving us, but we are not seeing it at that moment. The issues appear to be outside ourselves, caused by others, but are they?

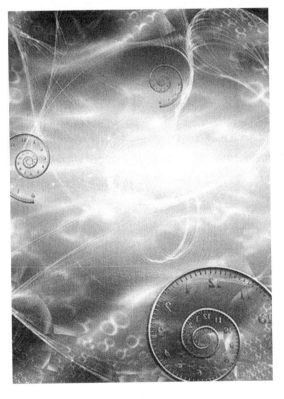

I have followed a cleansing practice while meditating or praying, where I look at a problem I am having, and I see if I can find the source of the problem by following the conscious thought backwards to the thought that preceded it. I refer to this as *"following threads"*. These previous thoughts will arise either through direct memory or through the help of spirit.

Once the thought is followed back to the source thought or original thought, I ask spirit to help with providing a solution and then release this issue to spirit.

For example, I was troubled once by seeing an elderly woman who was disabled. Having been left with an odd feeling, later during meditation I would look at this and ask, "*Why did it bother me that this woman was disabled?*" Then I would be quiet until I saw a path backwards to the source of that thought. In my mind, I heard that '*it was because I am looking at performing healing but felt a loss in confidence as to what to do, or how to apply this to her*'. Then I followed that thread and asked... "*Why am I not confident in my choice to perform healings?*" Again, I waited until I heard in my mind that '*part of me is not convinced that I am capable of any form of healing at all*'.

Seeing where my real problem lied, I wanted to find a solution, so I then followed that thread and asked... "*Why am I not more confident? What can I do to become more confident and get to where I know, and don't just hope?*". Again, I waited until I heard in my mind, '*I have to release a past image of myself and allow a new one to come forth*'.

Having followed this thread back to its source issue, I now have a task to perform, so I said "*The image I have of myself, my capabilities and my skills, I hand over to spirit to correct. I would rather see my true self as being capable and confident.*"

As you can see, the original thought that bothered me was a marker or beacon that something needed to be looked at, but that thought itself wasn't the problem. It was by following the threads of that thought backwards to the original thoughts that created it, that I was led to the reason or source of the problem.

Only when you work your way back to the source of a problem, will you gain ground and truly be moving forward in your spiritual walk. Think of it this way, if you only resolve issues that are on the surface, it's like putting a band-aid on a cut that will never heal, but if you dig deeper to find the source of the problem, you eliminate the cut altogether.

Today's Task:

Overall, the goal is to find an issue you have had with anything. It doesn't matter how large or small the issue may have seemed. They are all the same to spirit. Look at that issue, follow the threads back until you find something that can be corrected, and then hand it over to spirit for correction.

There is no single format to follow, but the basic premise for most issues can be found this way:

"Why did _____ bother me?"

Be still and wait to receive an idea of what thought was behind your reaction.

"Why did _____ matter?"

Be still and wait to receive an idea of what thought was behind your reaction.

Repeat those two base questions until you get to the source of the issue.

"The 'insert source of your problem', I hand over to spirit to correct. I would rather 'provide an opposite positive affirmation."

Track another thread.

Track another thread.

Today's quote from ACIM:

"Miracles are examples of right thinking. Reality contact at all levels becomes strong and accurate, thus permitting correct delineation of intra- and interpersonal boundaries. As a result, the doer's perceptions are aligned with truth as God created it." – ACIM T-1.I.37

Notes

Step #10 – Releasing Entanglements and Cords

We are energy. Everything is energy. Energy never ceases to exist, but simply transforms from one form into another. Energy flows, energy expands, energy envelopes and energy entangles.

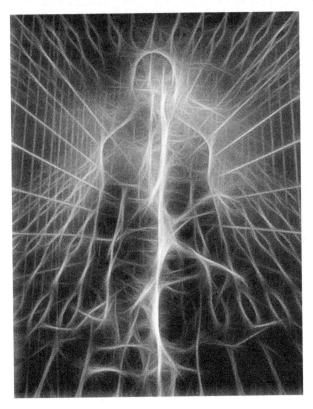

Entanglement of your energy field with another energy field is not necessarily a bad thing or a good thing, but it can be a hindering thing. As we look at undoing things to release our mind and spirit, the focus will always be on releasing those things that never were helpful or are no longer helpful. If something is being helpful, we let it stay there until it is no longer helpful.

When you invite spirit to work with you, your energy fields become entangled. When you reach out to anyone or anything, your energy fields become entangled. This is a natural state of energy. The problem that can arise is when this entanglement becomes constricted and does not release when it would have normally gone on its way.

These circumstances may resolve on their own as the energy slowly returns to its source, but meanwhile, you might not feel at ease. Maybe you have pain where you have no problem, or you are sad for no reason at all. This could be due to a recent entanglement with somebody or something and you are picking up on their energy characteristics. We would call this an unhelpful entanglement.

Sometimes, however, the entanglement does not let go at all and creates a permanent cord between yourself and the person or being. With no idea on your part, these cords could affect how you see things, how you feel about things, how you react to things, etc. This often explains why sometimes you feel motivated to do one thing or another without really knowing why. It could easily be that this motivation is not originating within your own thought system, but you are simply, and blindly, reacting to it. Again, this may or may not be helpful, so when looking to release such things, we focus on what never was helpful, or is no longer being helpful.

The reason I keep repeating the idea of selecting between the helpful or unhelpful connections is because you are not a victim. They were not set in place by force by anything outside yourself. If they are there, you either asked for them or simply allowed them, but they were never forced upon you.

A helpful entanglement could be where you asked for help in overcoming a problem, and it is in this entanglement with another being's energy and guidance that you overcome the problem. Alternatively, you may have opened yourself for an unhelpful entanglement while being angry, or during substance abuse, and an unhelpful energy connection could exist that makes your life more difficult than necessary.

Since there may be entanglements or cords that are helpful just as much as there are those that are not, it is not our intention to break all cords and connections. Our focus and intention will be on only releasing the ones that are no longer helpful and free ourselves from their influence.

Today's Task:

Allow your mind to quiet and say these two things:

"Any unhelpful entanglements that I am carrying at this time, I release to their source. I extend gratitude for what I may have experienced from them, but I would like to let them go now."

"Any cords that I have that are no longer helpful, I cut and release the energy to return to its source. I extend gratitude for what I may have experienced from them, but I would like to let them go now."

Allow some time for your request to sink in, and repeat the process two more times, for a total of three times. Provide enough pause between each request to reach a state where you mean it and are open to allow your request to be resolved.

Today's Quote from ACIM:

"God's creations never lose their holiness, although it can be hidden. The miracle uncovers it and brings it into the light where it belongs. Holiness can never be really hidden in darkness, but man can deceive himself about it. This illusion makes him fearful because he knows in his heart it is an illusion, and he exerts enormous efforts to establish its reality. The miracle sets reality where it belongs. Eternal reality belongs only to the Soul, and the miracle acknowledges only the truth.

It thus dispels man's illusions about himself and puts him in communion with himself and God." — ACIM T-1.I.31:4-11

Recommended Accessories and Services:

Energize Your Life with Reiki Spirit, Mind & Body Energy Work

Reiki energy has the capacity to provide healing on every level of your being, starting with your spirit, moving on into your mind and finishing up with the body. When Reiki energy work is applied to all aspects of your being, powerful healing is possible.

Schedule an Appointment at (https://www.deephealinglight.com/healing-services/sessions/reiki-spirit-mind-body-healing.php)

Notes

Step #11 - Opening, Listening and Receiving Guidance

The perception of our life's journey can be like the feeling you have while driving down a highway at night during blizzard conditions, where there is just a small area on your windshield that you can see through. You see almost nothing, and even what you do see is

fragmented and narrow, but it's just enough to get you by, which leaves you rather unsettled.

If your drive long enough like that, it just becomes normal. Your focus goes only to surviving and trying as hard as you can to make your driving decisions, even though you are practically blind.

Your life's journey was never meant to be that way. Why would you want to settle for such a narrow and dark perspective when you can choose to turn on your spiritual lights and wipers and see things so much more clearly? It is because you either don't see the option or don't believe the option is possible, but I'm telling you that the option does exist, and it is possible.

Spirit sees a much bigger picture and you can experience some degree of that bigger picture as well. Spirit is not restricted to obstructed windshield views like us, but more like popping off the roof and floating above the vehicle views where you can see everything.

Likewise, when opening and connecting to spirit, the fog in our minds that makes it difficult to make decisions or see a circumstance more clearly, can be lifted, parted or thinned so that our perception is much clearer, and life is no longer unsettling.

Opening your mind is the same as saying "*allow your mind*". It's about permission being granted to spirit to interact. It can be as simple as saying, "*I allow and welcome spirit to speak to me and through me.*" Or even simpler yet, "*I allow*".

Listening for what spirit says is a process of quieting your own thoughts and setting aside as much of your own thinking as possible. The beginning process is the same as already explained in Step #2 of this course. Once your mind is quiet, watch for thoughts that seem different or are more pronounced. You'll learn to more easily tell the difference after doing this for a while.

Receiving the actual guidance involves accepting what you are hearing and learning to decipher subtle changes to what we are supposed to be hearing due to our own filters that change the message. Because a part of us is so sure we are right, we don't always allow spirit to express themselves without modifying the thought. As time goes by, work on setting aside your ego and your own self-interests, then more direct guidance will come through.

When spirit does communicate to you, it could be something you hear, something you feel or something you see. This varies with each person, so initially, just be open for anything. Pay attention to anything you hear (not necessarily audible, but a louder or clearer thought in your mind), or anything you see (clearer or prominent images that stand out), or anything you feel (a sense of happiness, frustration, joy, etc.).

You will get better with hearing, feeling or seeing the messages over time if you practice being open to spirit. That's right, you must practice being open because even though you requested to be open, those are just words to start a process, but it takes practice for you to really mean it and to truly allow it.

Today's Task:

Open your mind by saying, "*I allow and welcome spirit to speak to me and through me.*"

Then, "*What would you like to say to me right now?*"

Quiet your mind and listen for what spirit communicates to you. Keep setting your thoughts aside and focus on a light or a sound.

Receive guidance. Allow yourself to truly hear what is being said or shown.

If you are not getting anything, it helps to start some form of movement. To do this, imagine a door. Open the door and walk through it and see where you go.

It may be almost like daydreaming, but not really. Let spirit take you on a little journey, listen, feel and hear what you can, and then try again tomorrow, and the next day, and the next day ...

Today's Quote from ACIM:

"Miracles are the transcendence of the body. They are sudden shifts into invisibility, away from a sense of lower-order reality. That is why they heal." – ACIM T-1.I.17

Notes

_____

_____

_____

_____

_____

_____

_____

_____

_____

_____

_____

_____

_____

_____

Step #12 - Extending Love, Light and Healing

Congratulations on making it to the end!

This lesson combines the essence of everything you have been taught and shows you how to take that wonderful next step towards connecting with spirit and healing yourself and anyone you choose.

Your core being is pure love, light, energy beyond our understanding. All the possibilities of creation are in there, so every potential answer and miracle is already in there, you just need to let it out.

Understanding that you are not alone is a pivotal concept to accept because when you can better grasp that you are so interconnected with all other life, you will see that you can never lose anything you give, because when you give, it all works its way back to you because all things are connected, across all distance and across all time.

For all giving, creating, or healing, distance doesn't matter, but neither does time. It works best if you could set aside any expectation for any specific period of time in which you would hope to see an answer or some form of results because this may limit how the answer can reach you. Just let thoughts of time and distance float away.

Whenever a healing is extended, it is received instantly, but this happens on a plane of existence we cannot yet fathom. How and when this healing trickles down through the layers until it manifests itself in spiritual, mental, metaphysical or physical way, is not relevant. It may be instantaneous, or it could take a millennium. Spirit works with all healing thoughts, and none are ever lost, but we often do not really know what we are asking for, so it is very important that you learn to trust that your request is honored. Trust that spirit sees your intention and is working with you to provide what is best at that time and determining what is best at what would be the perfect time.

For all healing, to truly receive, you must truly give. I am not referring to anything physical here, although it can work the same. You cannot give anything to yourself because you already have it, but you often don't see it or believe it, so in practicing or trying to give to others, you loosen up that grip on disbelief.

Would you like to be healed? Extend healing to somebody or something else. Would you like to experience abundance? Extend abundance to somebody else. What you would like to have for yourself, first give it to another. The only reason you want it is because you don't believe you already have it, but you can learn to see you do have it, and you will be healed.

See that giving and receiving run parallel to each other. As you give, you also receive. As you receive, you also give. It's simply how it works. You can neither win nor lose because you never had any true need in the first place. All needs are the result of us forgetting who we really are, so if you want to experience a true Deep Healing Light and extend that to others, forgive how you see the world. Forgive how you see yourself. Forgive how you see anyone or anything. Just let it be.

The miracle occurs when you release those things preventing the naturally occurring miracle from happening in the first place. Every one of us is a miracle, but we placed layer upon layer of guilt, ego, misinformation, fear and thoughts of lack on top of this wonderful miracle that we are. So, to bring forth a miracle, we just need to remove the layers that have obscured it, and it is already there waiting.

Today's Task:

All improvements are a form of healing, so today, choose an improvement you would like to experience, and select a person or being to gift this to first. To do this, you must sink into the core of your being and be as genuine as possible. Set aside judgments, conditions, circumstances, and just be in the moment.

Focus on the gift you have chosen to give and absorb that thought deep inside and then extend it out towards that person or being. Extend that thought as a deep penetrating light that has no boundaries and can penetrate any obstacle. That thought is a love thought. That thought will last forever and will provide healing. It will provide undoing, allowing the miracle to return.

Bathe your person or being with your deep healing light. Hold your focus there for a while and feel the energy flowing into your crown chakra and out of your heart chakra. Do this for a few moments and then step back for a moment to see that you already have what you have given, because you could not have given it otherwise, and so then accept it for yourself as well.

See your being transformed into white radiant light and allow its healing power to flow into every part of your being as well. Now see that you are doing both ... extending your gift out through your heart and receiving your gift through your crown at the same time. Just radiate. Radiate. Radiate to heal and be healed.

Do this for each problem you discover you are having.

Do this for everything where you believe you are lacking.

Do this to remember who your brother is and who you really are.

Do this to extend love for the sake of love.

Do this to extend peace for the sake of peace.

See your heart opening as it is bursting with white healing light and just extend that wherever you see a need, or wherever you wish to extend love.

This is love. Love is light. Light is healing.

You are love. You are light. You are healing.

Peace, Blessings and all my love to you. Namaste

Today's Quote from ACIM:

"Miracles are teaching devices for demonstrating that it is more blessed to give than to receive. They simultaneously increase the strength of the giver and supply strength to the receiver." – ACIM T-1.I.16

Notes

Step #13 - You Are Not Alone

This final step was added to provide one additional level of enlightenment for you. This step, however, requires you do nothing other than allow it, as it has already been done for you. This idea is based upon one of the primary teachings from "*A Course in Miracles*" that teaches:

*"I am not alone, and I would not intrude the past upon my Guest. I have invited Him, and He is here. **I need do nothing** except not to interfere." - ACIM T- 16.4*

Let that sink in. Re-read it several times. Just allow spirit into what you believe is your reality. Your higher self, angels, higher beings of light and more, are always there, have always been there and will always be there, but we just need to get ourselves out of the way and simply let them in.

This leads into why I added a step 13 to a 12 step course. According to Doreen Virtues book on numbering, the number 13 indicates:

"The ascended masters (such as Jesus, Quan Yin, and so on) are with you, helping you maintain a positive outlook. The number 13 signifies that female ascended masters and goddesses are also assisting you in staying positive." (1)

In other words, **"You Are Not Alone".**

One final thought for you to carry is this:

Many will say that God is in their heart ... that God is inside them, but consider this, nothing is outside of God because nothing exists outside him, so God is not inside you...

- You are inside God -

(1) Virtue, Doreen. Angel Numbers 101: The Meaning of 111, 123, 444, and Other Number Sequences (p. 13). Hay House. Kindle Edition.

Today's Task:

Let the universe in. Let spirit in, and then, if possible, see that the only reason this is possible, is because it is already inside you. There is nothing outside you. That is why all things are possible, because you are all things, as are all other things. You need ask for nothing, but just to allow it.

Today's Quote from ACIM:

"Miracles arise from a miraculous state of mind. By being one, this state of mind goes out to anyone, even without the awareness of the miracle worker himself. The impersonal nature of miracles is because the Atonement itself is one, uniting all creations with their Creator." – ACIM T-1.I.44

Bonus:

Added the next page to act as a quick reference you can photograph or cut out and place in any convenient location.

12 Steps to Deep Inner Healing

Quick Chart

Step #1 – Go to Your Quiet Space

Step #2 - Settle Your Thoughts and Relax

Step #3 – Clear Your Energy and Chakras

Step #4 - Connect with Your Guides, Ascended Masters and Angels

Step #5 - Accept Yourself as Being Worthy

Step #6 - Release Bindings, Bonds, Agreements, And Contracts

Step #7 - Release Your Guilt and Fear

Step #8 - Hand Over Your Thoughts to (Holy) Spirit for Correction

Step #9 – Follow Your Threads

Step #10 – Release Entanglements and Cords

Step #11 - Open Your Mind, Be Quiet, Listen, And Receive Guidance

Step #12 - Extend Love, Light and Healing

Step #13 - You Are Not Alone

Spirit, Mind and Body Healing - http://www.deephealinglight.com

Notes

About David Nelmes

David is a Reiki Master Practitioner, Author and Teacher

David was raised predominantly protestant but became significantly involved with evangelical and Pentecostal beliefs as a teen and young adult. Aspects of this stayed with him until the late 1990's, but then something within him started to shift and he began to see God differently than his lifelong beliefs had taught him.

David began to see a loving God who did not have requirements, did not use fear as a motivator, and did not demand worship or sacrifice. He began to see a truly loving God; an unconditionally loving God. His openness to this new line of thinking lead him to study the teachings provided by "_A Course in Miracles_", and a whole new world presented itself to him.

Almost immediately, David began writing articles about his experiences and how he was seeing things differently, but he had to spend many years working on opening himself to spirit to where he was able to finally break through many major blocks and re-identify himself as who he is today ... and the journey still continues.

A few of the books David has published are "_Seeing God ...perhaps for the first time_", and most recently, "_Breaking Through When Feeling Stuck ... And Not Getting Stuck Again_". Both books are designed to provide you with multiple levels of healing and aid you in seeing yourself and Spirit more clearly.

David has a genuine and powerful sense of healing, teaching and writing. His desire to share his knowledge about spirit and energy work has manifested itself through writing books and articles and developing courses and workshops. In addition, his energy healing services are a testimony to the quality and power of what he has to share, with so much more yet to come.

Here are a few words David would like to share with you...

I love that you found this web site because I know the information and services provided here can genuinely help you to the core of your being.

"I am here only to be truly helpful." This is a phrase from *A Course in Miracles* that I strive to live by. Whenever I have felt I lost my way or wonder why I am here; what my purpose is; I remember this: *"I am here only to be truly helpful."* The actual verse goes like this:

I am here only to be truly helpful.
I am here to represent Him who sent me.
I do not have to worry about what to say or what
  to do, because He who sent me will direct me.
I am content to be wherever He wishes, knowing
  He goes there with me.
I will be healed as I let Him teach me to heal.

- A Course in Miracles - Textbook Chapter 2, Part V, verse 18

I am a healer, writer, and teacher, and my happy goal is to share what I have learned and continue to learn. Many masters who have gone before us have great lessons and achievements, and I have learned that we partake and benefit directly from those experiences, even if they were not our own. I absorb and channel what I can from them, and I share this with you through writing, healing and teaching.

I encourage you to make use of my courses and sessions, read my articles and absorb what I share. As with me, everything you learn from another, compresses time and shortens our journey back home to source, and that's the whole point or purpose of our existence, to discover our way back to Source.

In closing, I would like to share this excerpt from an article I wrote a few years back that truly helps to summarize how I see our creator and spirituality overall:

There is nothing God requires that you do. There is no payment or sacrifice he requires or desires. There is no path to discover by racking your brain in trying to figure out what it is that God would have you do. There is no physical thing in the entire universe that you need to give God or to those who claim they follow God. There is only one thing that God desires from you and that is for you to **Be Willing**.

- **Be Willing** to see clearly.
- **Be Willing** to choose differently.
- **Be Willing** to set aside what the world has taught you.
- **Be Willing** to be what he would have you be.

Your willingness creates an opening in your being that allows the Holy Spirit to Do things. It allows the Holy Spirit to heal you, teach you and guide you. Learn to Be willing and you'll truly see what **God Can Do**.

- Excerpt from article: <u>In Everything You Do</u>

Peace and blessings, forward and backward,

Our spiritual courses, sessions, products and blog help stimulate your spiritual growth. By helping you to connect more easily to spirit, you can learn how to heal yourself and others.

Experience powerful healing with a Reiki Spirit, Mind & Body Healing Session

Reiki energy has the capacity to provide healing on every level of your being, starting with your spirit, moving on into your mind and finishing up with the body. When Reiki energy is applied to all aspects of your being, that's when powerful healing happens.

Experience an Effective Energy Healing with a Deep Healing Light Session

These life changing healing sessions invoke Master Hilarion and Sananda, along with your guides and angels, to provide an effective energy healing process for removing many of the obstacles that are blocking you from connecting more easily to spirit and your higher self.

You can start the course for FREE today to begin a journey that can and will transform your life.

Learn About Self-Healing with '12 Steps to Deep Inner Healing'

These guidelines will help you remember and discover the light in you that is already a healer. Just spend 20 minutes a day for two weeks to begin a journey that can and will transform your life where you can connect better with spirit and bring about healing for yourself or anyone you choose.

Get Past Feeling Stuck with Our Breaking Through - Live Video Sessions

Our Breaking Through process will help you break through whatever has you feeling stuck, so don't let anything stop you from receiving the healing you truly desire. To help you get past any step that you may be struggling with, consider using a Live Video Session.

Restore your Energy Balance with a Chakra Clearing & Alignment Session

Restore your energy balance by having your chakra energy cleared or aligned. Though similar to a Reiki session, the focus is only on balancing energy flow through your seven primary chakras, which places you back into a place where natural healing energy can flow again.

http://www.DeepHealingLight.com

http://www.HealingTouchShoppe.com

Sessions can be performed via distance or on site. Courses are provided online or via live workshops.

Products that can be very helpful to your spiritual growth and development

Chakra Healing Kit – Individual Chakra or Seven Chakra Collection

A Chakra Healing Kit can help you create the focus necessary to bring about true healing to your spirit, mind and body. Available individually or in a kit of 7, (1 for each chakra). Each kit includes:

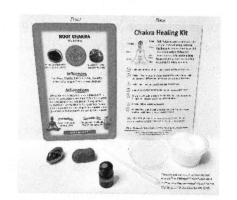

1 Chakra Card

2 Polished Crystals/Gemstones

1 Container with Cotton Balls

1 Micro Transfer Pipette

2 ml of Essential Oil

Detailed Instructions on Flipside

Chakra Healing Kit – Seven Card Collection

Chakra Healing Cards can help you create the focus necessary to bring about true healing to your spirit, mind and body. Learn how to restore your own chakras to a higher state of being with our Chakra Healing Kits.

The Seven Card Collection includes (1) card for each chakra for a total of 7 cards.

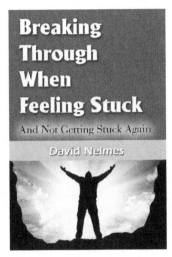

Breaking Through When Feeling Stuck

by David Nelmes

*Break through whatever has you feeling stuck. Regardless of the depth of your spiritual blocks, the **"Breaking Through"** process provided in this book is a real solution that will provide a path for your healing and help prevent it from happening again.*

Seeing God ... perhaps for the first time

by David Nelmes

Is God a God of love or a God of fear? I believe God is a God of love, so this book was written to clearly show that God is a God of love and that He does not teach through fear or use fear in any way. God is a God of peace. God is a God of harmony. God is a God of everlasting joy.

For more detailed information about our services, features and products, please visit our web sites:

http://www.DeepHealingLight.com

http://www.HealingTouchShoppe.com

Notes

Notes

Made in the USA
Middletown, DE
20 June 2020